———————————•———————————

YESTERDAY'S WATER
A CAREGIVER'S POEM JOURNAL

———————————•———————————

To Steve
fellow traveler
Sally

Sally Hubbard

9/100

CONTENTS

For Charles
June 4, 1931 - August 19, 2012

Charles Allen Hubbard, a 1953 graduate of the University of Houston College of Architecture, was happiest when overseeing the construction of mid- and high-rise buildings in the Houston area and in New Orleans. When not working, he created a sizable collection of black and white photographs of historic buildings and ruins, notably of the American Southwest and Greece, and marvelous watercolors of fall leaves and Tennessee barns.

The collateral damage caused by Hemochromatosis increased over the years, eventually involving his liver, pancreas, heart, and finally kidneys. —And inevitably, his personality, so that it was hard to remember who he had been when we met in 1971.

I offer this informal poem record of caring for Charles during his last year and a half to friends and strangers who are caring for chronically or terminally ill loved ones, in testimony that feeling numb, or disgusted, or abandoned, or inadequate, or lost, and grieving the loss of a person while he or she still lives, are understandable and acceptable. —That life continues, after the death of a loved one.

Somehow getting your perceptions into words, and sharing your experiences in a peer group, are invaluable. For creating a caregivers' support group at Otey Memorial Parish Church in Sewanee in 2012, my profound thanks go to Kathleen O'Donohue of folks@home, and to retired Episcopal priest Joe Porter, who guided the group through its first year. In the words of Sue Armentrout, an early group member, "Take care of the caregivers, or they will die first."

Sally Hubbard
Sewanee, Tennessee

DISENGAGED

It began to unravel the day the ICU doctor said "Go home.
Move your furniture around, make room for a hospital bed.
He will not be able to sleep lying flat again, ever.
I'll have a bed delivered this afternoon."

I stood at the foot of our marriage bed, and began to pull
the spread between the rice-carved posts toward me,
keeping it off the floor, gathering it into my arms;
then the sheets, the soft pad.

You need two friends, not even a screwdriver,
to dismantle an old bed. Pull the headboard free,
Lean it on the wall. Tilt the side boards to the floor.
Hold up the footboard; disengage the sides.

One by one, carry the parts upstairs.
Reassemble it for guests to use in another world.

October 2011

SPENDING AND SPENT

His breath steady and quiet
He sleeps soundly
I try to rest
Thunder and a brief shower
cause our dog to pace and salivate.
But they pass, she eats, we walk
in the polished light, the wet greens.
Still he sleeps
I try to rest.

To spend the day with someone
once meant to work all day, hike all day,
to visit and play together.

Now it means the light will be spent
The rain spent, the supper cooked
and partially eaten, the dishes washed
the evening hours passed, news watched,
The bedtime rituals of shot, snack,
pills, lotion completed
The day spent and non-refundable
The life circling in its holding pattern
spending, spinning, being spent
non-returnable, winding down down
till the red sun appears to slip
behind the mountain again
The dark watches begin
and another night is spent together.

May 18, 2012

STATUS CHECK

At 9 p.m. I walked outside, around my house
Found the Big Dipper in the north sky, the air still hot
A few lightning bugs out after curfew
No moon. Cicadas. Frogs jolly.
The bedroom curtains are softly closed
The dining room and kitchen windows
Are brightly lit. I stare and wonder
What is happening in that house.
The husband needs assistance to stand
Doesn't sit at the table
Rejects most foods, even old favorites.
Will eat only eggs, grits, and smoothies
made with fruit and protein powder.
He sleeps in his TV chair, in front of
Cajun Pawn Stars, alligator wrangling,
Duck Dynasty. (His father said
they were from Plum & Nelly—
plumb in the country and nearly in the swamp.)

The wife accuses herself of over-reacting
and under-reacting, since she's not privileged
to see his life line and where he is on it.
The right reaction is unknowable.
No ambulance came yesterday
but she questioned often whether she should
take him to the hospital. Bargains are made—
If he can eat lunch, then she won't take him.
If he keeps his meds down, then not this morning.

Maybe later in the day. If, then, if, then,
The washing machine runs most days
but there is no infant present
Laundry yes. Cooking no.
Dialysis yes, church no. Restaurant no
July 4th picnic and parade no.

The borrowed wheelchair is red,
his most favorite of all colors.
She needs to practice pushing him in and out
of doors that spring shut hard and bang the chair.
They need open doors, openings without doors
Someone guiding them through
Pushing when it's time to push.

July 8, 2012

THE FLYING TRAPEZE

"He flies thro' the air with the greatest of ease,
The daring young man on the flying trapeze.
His movements are graceful, all girls he does please,
And my love he's purloin-ed away."

My brother played the piano, my father sang with passionate angst
the circus song of 1868, con brillo, con gusto.
But when *The Greatest Show on Earth* came to our movie theater
In the 1950s, I was purloin-ed away.

For hours in the back yard, I hung from my knees, from my ankles.
Did back bends over banisters, back flips over pipes,
with pointed toes and long hair swinging.
Pretending to be tightly costumed, bright with sequins,
invincible, I was far above parents, brothers, school, town.

Now a trapeze hangs above my husband's bed
to help him move up an inch on the pillow, for him
to hold on with one hand, and push with the other to sit
on the edge till his feet find the floor.

But when he's settled, lotioned, covered with his quilt,
my muscles are still hard, my toes can point.
A chain book-reader, I float through time with the greatest of ease
To Istanbul in 1270, Florence in 1532, Mogadishu in 1990,*
Above our room, our house, as far as my eyes can take me.

March 27, 2012

*Anne Perry, *The Sheen on the Silk*; Irving Stone,
The Agony and the Ecstacy; Ayaan Hirsi Ali, *Infidel*

THERE'S MORE THAN ONE WAY

Nothing works today
Not Microsoft Word, not Email.
These magic tools bring projects—
articles to write, friends to answer
but, stalemate.
The cursor is still
perfectly centered in the screen.
At the end of my rope
I remember pen and paper
the telephone
tangible links
the solid social networks.
This material girl cries help
And help will come
But in the meantime
Begins to skin the next cat.

February 7, 2012

THREE DAYS, THREE NIGHTS

Monday was round and full of writing, reading, singing,
and good-natured attention to my husband's needs.

Why do nightmares invade that tear me open,
turn me inside out, my sweet fruit stretched apart
to be gnawed by rats and roaches?

Tuesday morning he said he had heard me sounding like a cat.
He had called my name but I did not hear. Screaming
in deep sleep is as hard as at the bottom of the ocean.

The day was round and full of writing, reading, exercise,
and good-natured attention to my husband's needs.

That night's dream began with a bridal couple
(me the bride) entering their bedroom with joy
and ended in full-out war in Syria, men shooting,

A baby torched, and me wanting to inflict as much
damage as I was capable of on an enemy, thinking
even asleep that I'd never felt that craving before.

Wednesday was round and full of reading, vacuuming, cooking,
and good-natured attention to my husband's needs.

I prayed on my knees to be relieved from night terrors.
My husband said "Sweet Dreams. That's an Order."
I dreamed that my daughter-in-law who finished a 150-mile

MS ride last weekend on a team that raised $23,000 was
a country music star, doing the sound check before a performance
in a red western hat and boots and sequined costume.
She saw me from the stage, called Sally! and came down to hug me.

April 25, 2012

WEDDING RING

Some days I do not wear my wedding band
As a way of noticing what is choice versus what is obligation
What is for personal reason versus what is contractual;
To honor by its absence on my finger
The solitary road I didn't realize I was taking at the time.

April 23, 2012

WHAT NOW

What now. Dear gods, what now?
The yard is mowed and raked
Flowers deadheaded
Laundry done
The bathroom glasses are clean.

Closets could be sorted, straightened, vacuumed
Clothes could be given away
There are drawers better left closed

At the office my services are no longer needed.
A few more paychecks will come,
Irregularly, small, another menopause
At home my job is to wait and see
Watch and ask
Remind—shots and pills—
Remind again—shots and pills—
Listen at night for labored breathing
Soothe lotion onto scaly legs and pillowed feet
Kiss a cheek, lips, that have changed generations.

My husband sleeps and sleeps
If we go out he sleeps
If we stay home he sleeps

My brother, ten years older than me,
has also changed generations. Outlived his wit and humor
Do I have ten years left in my generation
What is it time to do? To quit doing?
The one thing I can imagine wanting to do
Is to study Erik Satie, train my fingers to play his whimsical melody.
Measuring sound at his piano, Paris, 1887,
he is the only person who can play this blank page.

September 2011

SOMETHING TO PUSH AGAINST

Always I need something to push against—
suffering in the quiet times, but steady
and more cheerful when times are rough.
When I was almost too old to do it
I bought a silver Specialized bicycle,
a helmet, soft seat, hard shoes.
Five years in a row I rode 600 miles
training for one annual charity ride
175 miles around north Texas,
to push away a chronic fatal disease
from my family from my door from my heart.

Almost always there is darkness to push away.
It changes names, diagnoses, treatments, prognoses.
Changes people even—the crisis of one relative preempts
concern for another. But when my husband feels well enough
to fry his own eggs, drive himself to dialysis
then I reel like a drunk, reach like a blind woman
for the walls and the door frame, for balance, for bearings
for purpose, sliding my feet for fear of colliding
trying to unclip from the pedals
and catch myself in time.

April 13, 2012

SLEEP SHEETS

So sleepy, we go to bed. He is warm.
I cover him with just the sheet, to just the hips
Lie in the next bed, hear him go to sleep in minutes
Try to relax as my modern dance teacher
First taught me on the high school gym floor
Letting go of tension from toes to crown ... then
From stomach to both sides ... then
From top of head to feet.
Finally I feel the sideways slide toward deep sleep.

At 2 a.m. I hear him wrestling around
Ask if I can help, turn on the light
He has a bit of sheet gripped in his hand, right side up
The rest is twisted three times around his body
Bound by the oxygen line like a bouquet
Secured with florist wire.
Bliss—My purpose is revealed.
I undo the arrangement
Cover him lightly with rose petals
Kiss his brow, turn out the light.
Slip sideways down into deep sleep.

April 16, 2012

SILLY ME

I keep making
This same mistake—
Thinking I will have
An hour's quiet
At my desk.

April 29, 2012

SENSES

Walking the Mountain Goat Trail with a friend,
the scent of roses brought us to a dead stop.
We were enveloped in the perfume of native Multiflora Roses,
barely visible, deep in the woods.

Watching the trail in front of my feet, listening
talking, being quiet, I entered a cloud of honeysuckle
perfume, stopped to find the vine, thank it.

These senses seem to take turns vying for attention
First smell then sight then touch. First hear then see
or not, since small birds with huge voices are
perfectly hidden in the limbs above us.

May 3, 2012

SAFE FOR THE MOMENT

In our bedroom the TV blares
Law & Order, hour after hour
The oxygen machine churns and chugs
The door is shut and I feel barred

If I retreat to the guestroom upstairs,
devise some meaningful work
my spirit shuts down gradually
He is absent from my evening

If an elder is weary and
Needs to nap with *NCS* for seven hours
in hat and coat and blanket
can I let him
Should I let him

What good is physical therapy
What chance is there of conversation
He is safe for the moment
I am the one complaining
What good is sarcasm
What point in slamming doors

November 5, 2011

RIPPLES

Age and illness have their own peculiar intimacy
Skin has become silky, and hair fine
When I sooth anesthetic lotion
up my husband's back
fine ripples move before my fingertips

At times I did not welcome
his soft nudge against my back
We were out of tune, not in sync
At times I was a bowl that
he filled brimming to overflowing

Now all disharmonies are in the distant past
The only urgency is thirst, pain, itching, fear
These same fingers touch his same skin
His same voice calls me
Wakes me

February 11, 2012

RELATIVES

Because insulin, cardiac stints, and dialysis extend life
but do not cure disease, I invited the relatives to visit
in the fall of 2010. And again in 2011,
thinking that could be my husband's last Christmas.

All relatives have their own thoughts, needs, regrets,
agendas, gratitudes. Many have come; some more than once.
What about the others? They squabble, make bold plans,
Don't return phone calls.

They hurt maybe. They are poor maybe.
But I don't doubt they could come if thoughts
didn't hold them back from committing.

What are my options? Leave it to them ...
Offer one roundtrip flight to each of them ...
Take no part in dramas ... listen ...
Let their father decide.

I asked him once before if I should arrange flights for them;
He said phone calls were enough. I'll ask again.

April 23, 2012

RELATIVES · PART II

What makes it daunting is what
they all may bring, if or when our
Respective Children come this summer.
While I focus on crisis care,
food management, bath safety,
morning pills, evening pills,
four shots a day, preventing falls ...
now I also remember
opportunities we as parents missed,
our pessimism and imperfect decisions.
I feel fear.

We failed the challenge of
combining families, despite our
partnership and commitment. Now
I can only offer time together,
strive to accept who each of us is today,
pray for best possible outcomes.
If only we could have searched out
each one's best potential
and provided what was needed ...
seen God within each one.
It's late and I still lack heart.

May 7, 2012

OPEN

The simple act of opening curtains in the morning
Feeding the ecstatic dog
Making strong coffee
Speaking gently —

After a day of illness
A calm night seems stupendous.
I prop the door open with my toe
And welcome day.

February 29, 2011

ONE WHOLE DAY

I spent the entire day on my son's front porch
after deciding it was the balcony of a cruise ship,
and I, a paying passenger, had nothing else to do.

Breathing in honeysuckle air
mild spring sun exploring my arm and leg,
I read one whole book, hearing bird song,
garbage trucks, recycling trucks,
watching a woman running her dog
the yellow translucence of new leaves,
the family dog's ears swiveling independently
toward each fascinating sound.

At home I would have swept the porch,
trimmed the hedge, picked up sticks and limbs,
Worried   Worked   Worried   Worked
but not here, not today.

April 25, 2013

NOT TODAY

I try to tell myself it's the same job—
Shaking a full diaper into the toilet,
Rinsing it in swirling cold water

Or

Scraping up a dog's accident,
Scrubbing carpet with a soapy sponge,
Stepping on a rolled towel to soak up the moisture
(you just hold your breath).

Or

Helping an 80-year-old man out of soiled pajamas
Stripping his bed, pre-treating each stain.

But

The smell is not infant, or dog,
Or my husband for that matter—

It is rot, decay. Maybe it is death. Living death.
Instead of rinsing, I burn the underwear with trash
In the back-yard barrel. Instead of sponging with foam
I drag the rug outside to be cleaned some other day.

October 2011

MY FRIEND ASKS: *WHAT IS SELF CARE?*

SEEING that the luminous green of new leaves
in early morning sun outside my window
turns the shaded trunks of chestnut oaks lavender

SEEING that Orion's left toe dances on the cross
atop the church tower ... that the Big Dipper stands
on the end of its handle, emptying everything

SWEATING on the elliptical machine until
my pumping heart opens my mouth for air

WEARING only shoes that don't hurt ... and walking
barefoot on clean wood floors

CHOOSING one item for me alone for the grocery cart

SINGING as well as I can at every opportunity

WRITING down what matters

LISTENING to the frog Cantor start up
the Spring Peeper concert after dark

REMEMBERING that when the Peepers are finished
the Katydids will begin

April 9, 2012

MATINS

Clean air
Bright light
Morning
Thanks

February 7, 2012

LOVE

Subsiding with repeated discouragement
Flowing with energy and optimism
Love is never stagnant or calm like still water
It tumbles building and recedes at low ebb.

June 2012

RAIN

A day of sitting
Thunder breaks above
Rain falls straight and even

July 2012

LOSSES, GAINS

In the surgeon's waiting room yesterday
we sat by a younger man with one leg
wearing shorts, with a urine bag
balanced on his bare knee.
Comparing is inevitable but error-prone;
either man could live longer than the other.

But my primary complaint of the day—
that my husband has no appetite ...
eats a half dozen bites at meals then
pushes his plate away ... has lost 40 pounds
in three months ... That my refrigerator is crammed
with leftovers that only the dog and I will eat—
shrank in shame.

Empty all the containers into one soup pot.
add broth and call it Hungarian Goulash.
Do you remember being on a Danube River boat
at breakfast when the elegant buildings
of old Budapest eased into view and
there was no time to run to our room for cameras?
At left the Royal Palace appeared on Buda's Castle Hill;
We docked near Parliament in Pest
on the right-hand shore. Sometimes to see
is the only option, to watch, to intend to remember.
We have been blessed past all deserving.

Our lovely Collie Sabina will eat most of what I cannot.
What Sabina leaves will add nutrients
to the compost heap. Nothing is wasted.

April 19, 2012

LISTENING

What would I do
without morning birds
and evening frogs.
They are more present,
closer to me than humans.
They require no translation,
Format, punctuation, questions.
No spell check.
Like a watercolor wash their voices
fill in the space around me
and arrive unfiltered, unedited
at my brain stem
and my soul center.

Whistling   cheeping   bickering
calling   trilling   chirping
In porch-rocker church this morning
with coffee, cereal, peaches
Vishnu, vishnu, vishnu
my skin and muscles and bones
are awash in bird talk—
Chattering   mourning   chittering
scolding that I am too close
to their feeders.
Breezes fill in between
their small bodies and mine.
I am not the least bit alone.

In the yard tonight
with paper and pencil
I listen for frog chants but
there is not one voice.
They are waiting silently for rain.
My husband too is quiet, weary,
his tongue too dry for words.

May 26, 2012

HOW DO YOU SPELL SUCCESS?

Showering without falling

Transferring from wheelchair to chair without falling

Clean underwear

Pills swallowed without gagging

A half cup of lunch eaten

A half cup of supper eaten

July 10, 2012

FOUR-TRAIN NAP

I read outside until the breezes and cool spring sun
make me drowsy. Inside, I stretch out under a light blanket
and slip toward sleep.

From the valley ten miles away a train vibrates my body
for a full minute as it approaches and labors through the old tunnel.
It's a silent, invisible shudder—I don't know if anyone else

feels it in this house. It seems a secret, that waves travel
through miles of limestone, sandstone, and dirt to shake my bed
on the plateau a thousand feet higher.

It pleases me and sifts me deeper into sleep. A second
and later a third train settle me more, like flour nudged
and shaken through a sieve. The fourth train wakes me.

The back door opens; Sabina lifts her head and listens.
Charles is home from dialysis, ready for his late lunch
of macaroni elbows, butter, and garlic. Ready for his next nap.

Only in winter when leaves are down and winds are from the west
do we hear the prolonged klaxon blast as trains
roll through Cowan and up the incline into the tunnel.

I marvel at this also—that the sound waves of a 180-decibel horn
can be absorbed and stopped by tulip poplar, oak, maple, walnut leaves—
fragile, almost weightless, just a few cells thick.

May 11, 2012

DEAR DENTIST

Mercy, what can I say?
It's a relief to have a dental appointment.
To say goodbye, close the door,
Back out, start a CD, loud—
A Beethoven piano & cello sonata.
A relief to drive 40 miles in rainy fog
at 39, 42, 37 degrees, depending
on what bank you pass.

In the waiting room under stacks of *Car & Driver*,
I spy *Departures Magazine*
offering tours to Angkor Wat
Fourteen days, $2899.
That might be far enough.

January 13, 2012

AS FAR AS I CAN SEE

On Thursday, Friday, Saturday
My husband was dying.
Sunday, late, he resumed living.
I am buffaloed
My head throbs
One day dying
One day living
One day at a time.
My only choice, and my obligation
Is to begin the next right action
Do the next small right thing
Because tomorrow's job
Depends on today's.
Wednesday is decided by Tuesday
Not by me.

February 7, 2012

BOREDOM

Boredom develops silently
Like green slime in the birdbath—
Fecund, opaque, able to bear tadpoles
If ignored long enough.
But my agenda requires clean water.
I move them callously by the dozens
To the nearest runoff creek; wish them well.
Hose the basin out. Fill it sparkling full.
I never see birds there. Boredom may linger
In the concrete scallops, intolerable to birds.
The bowl is quick to stagnate;
Algae resume softly growing as the days warm.
If I put my face under, eyes open,
Chlorophyll might incubate new cells
In my obtuse pale brain, might cause something
To spawn and grow confidently, purposefully,
Incapable of idling, barely swimming even as it sleeps.
My fingers might stretch into the muck
To where plants meet concrete, to scrape and dig
For a different language, a new life form.

April 6, 2012

THE BREATHING MACHINE SONG

Sustain, regain, maintain, explain, complain,
Content, extent, recent, decent, repent,
Annoy, deploy, enjoy, destroy, ahoy,
Desire, aspire, retire, expire, rewire.

Expound, rebound, abound, surround, around,
Suspend, append, rescind, pretend, depend,
Repair, despair, prepare, compare, declare,
Detain, terrain, domain, cremain, remain.

(2 quatrains of iambic pentameter)
April 2, 2012

COFFEE

Two mugs of water touch in the microwave—
One from the Alexandria library in Egypt, for him;
One from the music festival in Sewanee, for me.
After 38 years and intractable illnesses
Still he makes our coffee most mornings, heats the cups,
Feeds the dog, lets her out, comes back to bed.
He can't carry the full mugs now,
Leaning so heavily on his curved wood cane.
I bring them, open the drapes, lean back on my pillow.

Our visit time evolved from late afternoon cocktails
To early morning coffee more than 20 years ago.
But now we are in two beds, his hospital bed beside
The twin bed I inherited from my grandmother.
With his head raised, I can't see his face.
Our outlooks are parallel—
Possibly, or not, facing a common thought.
And there's almost no talk other than *I'm sorry, what?*
Still, drinking coffee together is something—

A sacrament requiring no new, or old, words
Quietly consecrating each new day together.

May 14, 2012

90-DAY REVIEW

Ninety days of dialysis means 180 hours of removing, filtering, returning blood, plus adding vaccines and hemoglobin boosters ... watching 180 hours of cooking shows, fishing shows, Antiques Roadshows, How It Works, CSI. Pleasant interchanges with excellent nursing staff. Dozing. Minimal conversation with others doing the same.

My appointment with his doctor was at 1 but now it's 2
No matter. The afternoon belongs to Charles
Time has changed. We sleep more, eat less
Talk little. I carry a sense of instant availability
Twice while I held his right hand he has pitched forward
and I've stopped his falling. By the time I imagine
his calling out and colliding with concrete,
he is vertical again.

For two years I've read any book that interested me
About one per week, intent on escape—
Now that has no appeal. I don't want to waste an hour
reading other people's stories.
That sense of needing to pass the time is gone
Replaced with needing to write
With this change
come more days of more happiness

Now I can tune to my one true station,
where poems come from through that membrane,
that drum head, pure energy on one side
words on the other. Source of joy.

Our new doctor mentioned the possibility of cancer
And ordered tests and x-rays. Congestive heart failure,
Diabetes, kidney failure, and cancer? If that is true,
We will walk through it one day, to next day, not asking
Why or why not. The why's and why not's are as
Permeable, as porous as a wet window screen.
It's too late for explanations.

May 3, 2012

WATER CRISIS

More than weight and muscle loss
Or limiting potatoes, beans, spinach
Or giving up tomatoes and okra and dairy
Or treatments requiring more than 15 hours a week,
The hardest part of hemodialysis is thirst.

My husband has drawn a line around a pitcher
To indicate 32 ounces of water,
His limit per day—including to take pills.
He's cut back making soups, says no thanks
To vegetable juices and protein smoothies because
He craves 32 ounces of pure clear water.

When he asks for frozen grapes, crushed ice,
Mouth-moisturizer spray, there is near-despair in his eyes.
If I start to remove a nearly empty glass from the table,
He grabs for it. *Let me have that!*

We've always honored and cherished water.
On his childhood farm an artesian well
Spouted cool water year round.
His father built a windmill to pump
Well water up to the tank.
When I was a child we expected to run out of water
In August, and filled bathtubs with rusty water
For each day's use.

In Colorado we had only native plants and trees
And never watered them. We didn't let water run
While we brushed our teeth or soaped dishes.
When we camped at Keet Seel, water dripped from a spring
Into the spout of a covered blue-enamel coffee pot.
After we filled our water bottles, it took several hours
To re-fill. In Arizona we turned the shower off
While we shampooed our hair, and on again to rinse.

We always valued water. Seeing anguish
In his eyes because dialysis removes four liters of water
From his body is abhorrent to me. I want to
Give him tall insulated glasses of ice water.
And a quart of coffee, not a half cup.
Cold soups in hot weather. I want to say
Ignore the rules! Drink to your body's content.
Where water is clean and plentiful
It is cruel to deny it.

But at present he believes compliance is worth it.
Dialysis can take four hours instead of five
Without "excess" water in his system.
Treatment is easier; blood pressure doesn't plummet.
His will is more rational than his eyes.
He doesn't see them begging.

May 14, 2012

ENIGMA

Yesterday my husband told our priest, again,
that he was tired and ready to be finished
with debilitating weakness, with treatments.
What if—he stops medications, insulin, dialysis?
Then what, for how long? —for him, for me?

He and I had both signed Advance Care Plans saying
that we do not want CPR, artificial life support,
surgery, transfusions, or tube feeding, when "quality of life
becomes unacceptable and conditions are irreversible."
But treatments accumulated, and here we are

Barely afloat in artificial life support and irreversible illness.
With best intentions we crept too far into white-capped swells
beyond our depth. We strain to touch bottom.
Yesterday we dredged up words to consider how and why
(when breakfast is life's only pleasure) stopping is not suicide.

Today he made coffee and supervised breakfast: three eggs
turned quickly, chopped and mixed with peppered grits.
What I see—is compliance with medication schedules
and treatment. The daily effort to continue life.

I ask him how to reconcile what he said
With what I see. His answer:
I can do both. Both are true.

June 19, 2012

69

COLOR CIRCLES

Two pieces of jewelry, both bought for myself—
One a gold bracelet to mark fifty years
Of slowly growing up since high school graduation,
The other a necklace worn for the first time today
To honor 38 years of marriage.

Small, semi-precious stones repeat around my neck,
celebrating beauty in diversity,
Grace in adversity, life in daily variation,
Lives linked with mine since childhood.
Lavender amethyst like sunset, thought to signify sincerity,
Is for February, especially for my intriguing grandson
And my mother's death.

Blue topaz is for clear skies, for loyalty,
For November and my middle brother.
Garnet, red for January, warms midwinter
And means constancy and my loyal younger brother.
Citrine is yellow for sunlight and Blackeyed Susans—
My Friday color. Peridot, lime green, is for August,
For friendship and my grandmother.

Three stones do not revolve here—
Ruby, for July, for freedom, for my firstborn, my daughter;
Sapphire for September, for truth, for my son; and
Pearl for June, for wealth, for my husband of 38 years.
These form a sturdy constellation in my sky,
Circling the Polestar, unremovable.

Bought for myself, why?
Who else would know my circles of color
In shadow days? My husband's eyes are closed
Riding beside me to dialysis. He is too tired
For shopping, for surprises, even for anniversaries.
He has stopped carrying cards or cash or keys
Because it takes all his strength to carry himself
There and back, there and back, there and back.

June 15, 2012

SPOON DUTY

We feel foolish but we get used to it—
Walking across the living room with an empty tablespoon,
Filling it heaped and rounded with mayonnaise,
Walking it back for Charles, in his TV chair, to lick
Like an all-day sucker. Nothing else relieves his thirst.

Spooning used to mean to curve and conform
Our bodies like nesting silverware.
Spoonerism means accidentally transposed words
Like, *make us needful of the minds of others.*
Madame de la Sauce Mayonnaise used to mean
My father reading poetry out loud.

But this is not for tenderness or entertainment.
Spoon duty moistens his tongue, allows him
To swallow and to speak.

July 16, 2012

INSEPARABLE

What was it about the light today
outside Lost Cove Cave? A creek runs out of the alcove
over mossy rocks and comes into bowl-sized pools
in the creek bed, in rivulets sparkling with light—

Reflected light I know—from that ferocious dying sunstar
93 million miles away. But the pools seemed self-luminous,
electrified with strobes and strings of white tree lights
looking at me, focused on me. Me, today.

I've walked there so many times when leaves and clouds
choreographed dappled light-shows across the cliffs
but today I was there in it, in cracks and crevices
with the bonsai ferns.

We stepped carefully through butterflies—Blue Swallowtails,
Coppers, and Spring Azures with their pairs of
hinged lavender wings, small as a toenail, opening
and closing, opening and closing, without any visible body.

I was with friends, but also not with them.
Normally butterflies would be doing their busy duties
unaware of my presence, but we were one, today.
My skin did not exclude me, hold me apart.

On the trail exquisite clusters of wild flowers stood still
at my feet to receive me. Wild Azalea, Rhododendron,
Mountain Laurel glowed under the leaf canopy. I wonder
if it's always like this, inseparable, and I don't know it,

Or whether some switch in the great scheme of things
was set wrong today and what should be human and
what should be wet or light ray or wing or bird calls were all one.

Is it because that silk curtain between life and death
seems close to my husband now
that I was given a few moments of seeing beyond this side?

April 29, 2012

IN CASE

I hope I didn't hear
What I just heard
But go quickly to look
In case his knee gave way
And his tall body fell tree-like
Beside the wingback chair
And he cannot get up.
In case his son heard the crash too
And will come running downstairs
In case it takes two to lift him up.

July 10, 2012

HIS SKIN, MY SKIN

In the first week, hemodialysis removed 30 pounds
of fluid from my husband's bloated body.
It continues three times a week to shave away muscle mass.
His arm is like my wrist; his calf the size of my ankle.
His legs can barely, briefly, hold him up.
The flat tibia's sharp edge is center-front,
covered as by a wrinkled burlap sack.
I massage his legs with lotion every night—
as before when they were stretched round—
wondering what good it can do.

He was 40 when we met. The photo on my dresser
shows him at a picnic on the levee with my children,
aged 4 and 5. He tossed cherry tomatoes up and caught
them in his mouth. He charmed us.
Last night somehow his face was that face
without years or illness. Handsome. I told him so.

This is what lotion can do—
(Even when his face does not mirror the photo)
It can touch, hold, reach, calm
the person who is still there.
It can remind me who we were.

April 5, 2012

EXTENDING LIFE, PROLONGING DEATH

I want Hugh to live, dearly, dearly do I want him to live, if he can be returned to real life. But I do not want dying (rather than living) to be prolonged for him. Over and over we have promised each other that we will not let this happen ...The medical profession is at a time of crisis because of the amazing instruments of modern medicine. They save lives. But they also prolong dying horrendously.

Madeleine L'Engle,
Two-Part Invention: The Story of a Marriage

How strange it is to live in a time when doctors preserve the lives of premature babies, damaged beyond repair, oblivious and having no vote. —When they place the burden of deciding whether or when to die on an 81-year-old man with numerous fatal illnesses.

As much as I can, I think of stepping into my husband's shoes and his reality: that if I stopped taking insulin and medications for heart and kidneys, and stopped dialysis, I could die in two or three weeks. Would it feel massively unfair? Someone smarter should make such an important decision! Could I rationally have conversation with everyone who matters to me most, and then pick the stopping moment? Do anyone's veins run with that much ice water?

When she was defeated by cancer, my friend Kitty denied herself food and IV fluids, and chose only pain patches and hospice care. As much as I loved and respected her, I was silently outraged, as though she had no right to end her life. Or I could not bear her courage, or her faith, that death was not the end, was just the next step. She was just going home ahead of us, and didn't owe us any explanations. Her body. Her life. Her next life.

I know nothing of a next life. I know only two things: That the components of my body came from exploding stars; That all life interconnects—the water and light at Lost Cove Cave, butterflies, flowers, my eyes and senses, ferns, leaves all express one truth: Life. Shared and continuing Life.

May 14, 2012

LAST IS JUST A WORD

that comes to mind more often now
—The last time my brother and his wife
will come to dinner
—The last time my husband and I
will go to church together
will sit with them, sing harmony

Meanwhile footsteps become more hesitant
and each day brings a different challenge—
a new puzzle to solve, decision to make.

For a few days Charles parked his wheelchair
and used his walkers, especially the new favorite
with three wheels and bicycle brakes.
Then back to the clunky one,
square, more stable, yellow tennis balls on its feet.

Now only the wheelchair can be trusted
to get him from bed   to toilet
to car   to dialysis   and I'm barely strong or balanced enough
to raise him in between, my body learning new ways
to reach, to brace, to support his weight.

I run warm water and place the shower mat and chair.
He creeps in—stooped, with bent knees—
and I think, Last Shower.
True or false? Just words, a freeze frame,
that make me pause and note a moment.

July 23, 2012

HOSPICE, DAY ONE

Every half hour is an hour
Two hours are four
My watch says 1 p.m., early afternoon
I was expecting 5!
The dialysis people required a full cardiac workup
(worried about fibrillation and low blood pressure)
But the stress tests may have been the last straw
He begged to stop the machine, to go home

"Adult Failure to Thrive" is the Hospice admitting code.
Not everyone can endure dialysis.
Or was the antibiotic for pneumonia
and bladder infection the final blow,
making him so nauseated he stopped swallowing
food or medications. No longer interested. Tired.

What we did to help ... defeated him
best I can tell, today. But, no. Infection,
heart and pancreas and kidney damage
defeated him. We could not prevent it
though we delayed it for years,
long enough for the children to reach middle age
and come to him in peace.

August 6, 2012

HOSPICE, DAY TWO

That first thought when I find him
Contorted in dry heaves
Has to change
From what can I do and who can help
To
Accept. Think about pain control
(that doesn't cause nausea).
Changing directions from forward to reverse
Requires stopping
I don't need to take him anywhere
No one can fix it

One thing I acknowledge: doctors, stents,
Insulin, meds, and dialysis
Have held back death for decades.
In this week of refusing food and meds
Everything has begun to change.

His bed is not safe or soft
Until the sun is high and
Sabina and I are moving around him
Talking the way a dog and woman can.
Only then will he turn the TV off,
Struggle out of his worn, black leather Eames chair
Fall onto his pillow
Rest on his side
And sleep.

August 7, 2012

YESTERDAY'S WATER

The eight-sided glass
is full of clear water
A blue straw refracts into zigzags
and spots of blue glow.
The Hospice nurse questions me—
Is he dry
Have his bowels moved
What was his blood pressure this morning
His pulse   His respirations   His glucose
(I have only in the last two weeks
learned to give insulin after 26 years of shots)
Did he eat
Has he drunk

I answer what I can
He ate two pieces of penne pasta
Two baby limas

That's yesterday's water.

August 16, 2012

READY, NOT READY

In spite of months of preparation
I was slow to understand that
the day of birth had come.
I leaned against the merchandise displays
at Sears and felt tired before
my daughter came that night.
SMH, 1966

I knew from his raised eyes that
Charles was in a coma in his reclining chair,
His round mouth set in rictus,
His jaw locked wide open
For the most possible air.
I had no sense of his absence,
No expectation of change.

I closed my book, moved closer
Started reading aloud from the Book of Common Prayer.
Glorify the Lord, O mountains and hills,
O springs of water, whales, flocks, herds,
Glorify the Lord. I murmured Psalms and Services—
Ministration at the Time of Death, Burial of the Dead,
And An Order for Marriage, to hear those words again.

His steady agonal breaths continued.
I started on the hymns, singing softly
The day thou gavest Lord is ended,
The darkness falls at thy behest;
To thee our morning hymns ascended,
Thy praise shall sanctify our rest.

Familiar hymn after familiar hymn.
His granddaughter held his hand.
Friends came and stood at his feet
We talked quietly and so did not realize
For a moment that
His breathing had ended.

January 8, 2014

PLEASE RECYCLE

My friend asks: do you ever cry?
Do you miss him?
I dread answering,
Fearing offense or rejection.

No, no crying.
Not yet, missing him.
These days I am a crumpled knot
Of heavy-duty aluminum—
Stained, scorched, crushed
Into a thousand creases

But not discarded.
I am needing to open, unfold, be scrubbed and dried,
Knowing that the wrinkles will never disappear,
Hoping usefulness remains.

October 4, 2012

NIGHT TERRORS

The children surround and shout at me
You don't care
You're a fraud
Everything you've done is from obligation
Not from love

After a blustery night river birch leaves
Are strewn the length of the porch
Some green peppered with yellow spots
Some blotched half yellow, half green
I have changed our bedroom
To a sitting room—too fast
I don't miss him. They will know.

I changed colors overnight in a storm

I've dreamed and waited months to do it
I've hung more of his watercolors but
Had to be told to place photos of him
On the dresser.
Changing roles requires dying
Our marriage died
His bride   his wife   died with him

I will live here now.

August 22, 2012

JUST BEFORE WAKING

Just before waking I heard him calling

SALLY!

YES!

My instant response out loud woke me up

Recognizing everything about the voice, then

Remembering that I had responded with kindness every
single time

Remembering that I am free of that necessity now.

September 13, 2012

RETURNING

My friend is here
Our coffee mugs are by the fire
We sit in rocking chairs
We laugh.

She has brought three fragrant wreaths
From the North Carolina mountains
We hang them above the mantel,
On the back door and

On the front door
So friendship will come in
And darkness stay out.

Until she came I debated hanging even one
To bless my going out and my returning.

December 12, 2012

TEARS

If tears could come
They would run down soft mossy shingles
Like summer rain, drip from wide eaves
Onto pine needles, soak into sandy loam
All afternoon, all evening,
Fragrant through the night.
The ground would never dry out.

March 1, 2013

In *Yesterday's Water*, Sally Hubbard allows us to accompany her as she negotiates the loss of her beloved husband of nearly forty years, Charles. In unflinchingly frank language that, ballet-like, is equally remarkable for its delicate grace and its contained power, these poems chronicle an extraordinary love challenged by looming mortality and the agony and drudgery of debilitating disease for both the dying and the caregiver. Resolutely refusing easy solutions to the mysteries of living and dying, Sally Hubbard's poems nevertheless recover and celebrate the complex beauties and comforts of imperfect human love and its ability to nourish and sustain our spirit.

Logan Delano Browning,
Editor of *Studies in English Literature, 1500-1900*

This wholesome collection is full of sensitivity, passion, compassion and empathy. This is the brave record of the real journey of a lost loved one and the true but always hidden life of the care-giver. *Who cares for the caregiver?*

Professor Grace Muwanguzi Kyeyune,
Founding Rector of Hope University, Semuto, Uganda

Sally Hubbard's beautiful poems and courageous, honest report—with its long darkness and flashes of light—will help many people understand the caregiver's journey.

Barbara Hughes,
Author of *Enfolded in Silence*

Beautiful. The habit of charity, caritas, agape, is hard-won in the opportunities of real life. These poems provide a deep glimpse into that painful and glorious adventure.

Robert Hughes,
Author of *Beloved Dust: Tides of the Spirit in the Christian Life*

In poems like "Something to Push Against," with respectful humor Sally Hubbard has pushed against the walls of despair, hopelessness, and feelings of inadequacy that beset us when our loved ones are terminally ill and dying.

The Reverend Gideon B. Byamugisha
Co-founder of the African Network of
Religious Leaders Living with AIDS
Founder of Hope Institute and Hope University, Uganda

The raw truth of life and death with their beauty and distress, compassion and detachment, emotion and numbness all are fully evoked in the words and images of these poems. As I sped on in anticipation of the next poem, my mind filled with the images of my loved ones who are in need of words; who need to hear their own truth so clearly and eloquently stated.

Kathleen O'Donohue,
Director, folks@home

Made in the USA
Charleston, SC
09 May 2015